WELCOME
TO THE
WEIRD WORLD
OF
GLEN BAXTER

also by Glen Baxter

WELCOME TO THE WEIRD WORLD OF GLEN BAXTER

Glen Baxter

PERENNIAL LIBRARY

HARPER & ROW, PUBLISHERS, NEW YORK
Grand Rapids, Philadelphia, St. Louis, San Francisco
London, Singapore, Sydney, Tokyo, Toronto

Several of the drawings in this collection have appeared in *The New Yorker.*
Copyright © 1989 by The New Yorker Magazine, Inc.
Grateful acknowledgment is made to *The New Yorker* for permission to reprint.

FIRST EDITION

Library of Congress Cataloging-in-Publication Data

Baxter, Glen.
    Welcome to the weird world of Glen Baxter / Glen Baxter. — 1st ed.
        p.   cm.
    ISBN 0-06-096388-8 (pbk.)
    1. American wit and humor, Pictorial.   I. Title.
NC1429.B34A4   1989   88-45922
741.5′942—dc20

89 90 91 92 93 MPC 10 9 8 7 6 5 4 3 2 1

Dedicated to the genius of
Richard Griffin

From the Pages of History

IT WAS A SMALL VOTIVE BUST OF
CONNIE FRANCIS.....

ROBIN WAS CERTAINLY IMPRESSED WITH
THE SIMULATED TEAK FINISH

YOUNG ARTHUR'S EARRINGS WERE
THE TALK OF NOTTINGHAM

IT WAS THE SMALLEST PIZZA THEY HAD
EVER SEEN

"NOT SO FAST, VARLET — I DEMAND A SECOND
FITTING!" BELLOWED SIR PEREGRINE

FRUITS OF THE WORLD
IN
DANGER

Number 12   The Kumquat

SIR ROLAND TRIED TO CONVINCE THE
SCEPTICS OF THE POTENTIAL OF HIS
LIGHTWEIGHT "MINI-SHIELD".......

IT WAS HUNGARIAN COOKING ALL RIGHT

GREAT FAILURES
OF OUR TIME

Nº 16

The First Yo-Yo

HAMMOND OUTLINED THE RUDIMENTS
OF HIS DARING ESCAPE PLAN

GREAT FAILURES
OF OUR TIME

No. 160 The First Pencil Sharpener

"BUT......I...ORDERED THE
CHICKEN KIEV..." BLURTED COOPER

ESSENTIAL SUPPLIES WERE
DROPPED TO THE BRITISH
AGENTS

"I'LL THANK YOU TO STOP JUGGLING MY
GHERKINS!" SNORTED THE ANGUISHED THROGUE

"WE'VE ONLY ENOUGH OLIVES
LEFT FOR THREE MORE MARTINIS,
SIR...." QUAKED LAWSON

HE SPOKE FERVENTLY OF HIS
VISION OF A CHAIN OF MULTI-
LEVEL PANCAKE HOUSES
IN EVERY MAJOR CITY IN
THE NETHERLANDS....

GREAT FAILURES
OF OUR TIME

No. 6 The First Parachute

"CAN'ST THOU NOT SEE IT, MY LIEGE?
'TIS BUT THREE BLOCKS NORTH
OF THE DELICATESSEN..."

GREAT FAILURES OF OUR TIME

*No.77 First Dental Extraction
by Red Admiral*

IT WAS RUDOLPH'S TURN TO
LUBRICATE THE CINDERS

GREAT FAILURES
OF OUR TIME

No. 226 The First Fly Swat

TUESDAYS, WEDNESDAYS
AND FRIDAYS....

GREAT FAILURES OF OUR TIME

No. 19 *The First Corkscrew*

GREAT FAILURES OF OUR TIME

No. 242 *The First Hula Hoop*

GREAT FAILURES
OF OUR TIME

No. 23   First Transatlantic Crossing

"CAN'T YOU SEE, BIGGS, THAT WHAT
WE HAVE HERE IS ALMOST CERTAINLY
EVIDENCE OF SOME PRIMITIVE FORM
OF TAKE-AWAY FOOD SERVICE...."

GREAT FAILURES
OF OUR TIME

No. 224 *The First Frankfurter*

BY NIGHT WE WOULD MARVEL AT
HIS DEXTERITY WITH THE SPONGE

SIR HENRY OF HAWKSWOOD
TENDED TO PREFER A WALL-
MOUNTED SWIVEL ARM FITTING
WITH A PASTEL PLEATED SHADE

DURING A MOMENTARY LAPSE IN
CONCENTRATION, I EFFECTED MY
ESCAPE FROM MY CAPTORS...

HUBERT GAZED ON IN AWE AT
THE MORSEL

COUNTING BEYOND THREE HAD
NEVER BEEN HIS FORTE...

ALONE IN HIS MOMENT OF
RAPTURE, RALPH RETURNED
ONCE AGAIN TO CONTEMPLATION
OF THE GOURD

"CAN I TAKE IT THAT THE ELECTRIC LUTE
IS NOT TO YOUR LIKING, MY LIEGE?" QUOTH ROBIN

ALEC SENSED THAT LIFE SOMEHOW
WAS PASSING HIM BY....

JANET HAD OPTED TO FLY "TOURIST CLASS"

THERE, AS USUAL, WAS EDELSON, DELIVERING
HIS POST-STRUCTURALIST ANALYSIS OF THE
MODERN NOVEL TO THE PRIVILEGED FEW

MADDOX SCRUTINIZED THE WORM'S
PROGRESS

"THESE PANTS ARE WELDED STEEL,"
ANNOUNCED THE STRANGER

MR. BOTTOMLEY HELD VERY FIXED IDEAS
ABOUT INTERIOR DESIGN....

IT SEEMED TO AMUSE HIM, SO I
COMPLIED WITH HIS ODD REQUEST

DAYS CAME AND WENT — ANXIOUS DAYS IN WHICH
WINIFRED NEVER MENTIONED HER INCREDIBLE
EXPEDITION TO SEE THE GENERAL

UNCLE ARTHUR WAS GOING THROUGH ONE
OF HIS "DIFFICULT" PATCHES AGAIN

SLEEPING IN THE GUEST BEDROOM DID,
HOWEVER, HAVE ITS DRAWBACKS....

BEFORE PLATT COULD CROSS THE BALL,
THE BIG NUMBER FIVE LUMBERED UP
AND LASHED HIM WITH HIS QUIFF

THE DRIVER GRINNED AT THE
OBVIOUS TWINKLE

IT WAS AN OFFER SHE DARE
NOT REFUSE

HOW HE HATED SATURDAY
MORNING SHOPPING

GREAT
MOMENTS
IN HISTORY
Number 43
The First Omelette

IT WAS A MONDAY AFTERNOON JUST LIKE
ANY OTHER.....

"I SUPPOSE YOU'RE ALL WONDERING WHY
I'VE GATHERED YOU HERE TODAY"
WHISPERED THE BOSUN

GERARD INSISTED ON FLAUNTING HIS
REVOLUTIONARY THERMAL SNOOD

IT WAS THE FOURTH TIME THAT DADDY HAD
FALLEN FOR THE EXPLODING FORK ROUTINE......

THERE WAS A HINT OF TRIUMPH IN
UNCLE FRANK'S BLUE EYES

THERE WAS GENUINE CONCERN IN
DAPHNE'S FRANK BLUE EYES

THE NURSE ENTERED WITH THE
BRIGADIER'S CALORIE—CONTROLLED
BREAKFAST.....

ALTHOUGH THERE SEEMED TO BE
A GENERAL LACK OF AMENITIES
I WAS FORTUNATE ENOUGH TO HAVE
BEEN MY GIVEN MY OWN BED...

"WE'RE IN LUCK. THE ENTRANCE
TO THE SAFETY DEPOSIT VAULTS
IS ONLY PATROLLED EVERY
HALF HOUR!" GROWLED CELIA

WE ADVISED HIM AS TO WHERE
HE MIGHT PLACE HIS HERRING

WITH
COLONEL
BAXTER
IN THE
FOOTHILLS

FRANK'S WRISTWATCH WAS THE
SUBJECT OF A NUMBER OF VICIOUS
AND SEEMINGLY POINTLESS
ATTACKS BY LOCAL PESTS

"I'LL NEVER FORGET THE DAY M'BLAWI
STUMBLED ON THE WORK OF THE
POST-IMPRESSIONISTS...."

SYBIL GASPED. THERE ON N'BOTO'S
PALM WAS TATTOOED A PERFECT
STREET MAP OF DUNDEE...

IT WAS CLEARLY A PRIMITIVE DEVICE
FOR SHREDDING BEETROOT

"DIE SCHWIERIGKEIT IST, DIE
GRUNDLOSIGKEIT UNSERES GLAUBENS
EINZUSEHEN," NOTED NGOTOGO

THE DISTRICT COMMISSIONER'S MINT
TEA WAS HELD IN AWE THROUGHOUT
THE FOOTHILLS

RIDLEY WAS ROUSED EACH MORNING
AT 7:15 SHARP

THERE IT WAS — THE LEGENDARY BALL
OF SOOT OF THE XOACAPOTALX

I WAS OBLIGED TO ENDURE THE
ROUTINE KNEE INSPECTION

YOUNG ROSENBERG HAD PERFECTED A
METHOD OF COATING SHOELACES WITH TWO
THIN LAYERS OF UNSALTED BUTTER

"BUT I _AM_ THE POSTMAN!"
BLURTED NTONGA

BARTWELL SAW THROUGH THE DISGUISE
ALMOST IMMEDIATELY

AS ASHTRAYS GO, IT WAS
CERTAINLY QUITE IMPRESSIVE

"THIS DEFINITELY CONFIRMS THE EXISTENCE
OF AN EARLIER, MORE PRIMITIVE SOCIETY!"
BLURTED PENNINGTON

OUR CANADIAN
· COUSINS ·

IT WAS HARVEY'S BOLD PLAN TO ARRIVE
AT THE ENEMY HEADQUARTERS AT
PORT ARTHUR UNDETECTED...

THE GEOLOGIST SPENT MANY HOURS
REHEARSING THE GLOWWORM TROUPE

THEY WERE JUST ABLE TO MAKE OUT
THE LONELY FIGURE OF THE BASSOONIST

HELMUT CHECKED THE BOULDER AT TWELVE-
MINUTE INTERVALS THROUGHOUT THE NIGHT

"ANOTHER SLIM VOLUME OF MODERN
ENGLISH POETRY!" SHRIEKED JACOBSEN

IT WAS MRS. CRABTREE AND SHE WAS
IN NO MOOD FOR PLEASANTRIES

"IF A FACT IS TO BE A PICTURE IT MUST
HAVE SOMETHING IN COMMON WITH WHAT
IT DEPICTS," MUSED THREEVES

SPRIGG ALWAYS HAD THE SUET
MAILED FIRST CLASS FROM DRESDEN

THE NEAREST TAXIDERMIST WAS
STILL THREE DAYS' MARCH AWAY

KEN WAS KNOWN TO GO TO
EXTREME LENGTHS IN THE
PREPARATION OF HIS SYLLABUBS

"WHAT HAVE YOU DONE WITH MY
WIMPLE?" GROWLED BIG 'BULL' HARPER

FRUITS OF THE WORLD
IN
DANGER

Number 1   The Orange

THERE WAS NOTHING ERIC LIKED
BETTER THAN AN EVENING ALONE
AT HOME WITH HIS TWINE

THE DEBATE OVER OWNERSHIP OF THE
RISSOLE DRAGGED ON WELL INTO APRIL

EMILY AND GWEN SPENT
MANY A HAPPY EVENING
COMPARING FISTS

"BUT I CAN SURE BROIL A
DING-DANGED SWELL STEAK"
RETORTED DORIS

OTTO OFTEN ASTOUNDED
UNWARY VISITORS WITH
HIS CATERPILLAR COLLECTION

RALPH'S DISAPPEARING WRISTWATCH
TRICK STILL REQUIRED A CERTAIN
AMOUNT OF FINE TUNING

BERYL HAD HIT UPON A WAY
OF RELIEVING THE TEDIUM OF
MISS ABERGHAST'S LESSONS

"I SENSED THAT BRENDA WAS TRYING
TO IMPRESS ME....."

IT HAD BEEN SUSPECTED FOR SOME TIME
THAT MAVIS WAS EXPERIMENTING WITH
A COMBINATION OF BALKAN AND
TURKISH BLENDS

"GOING DOWN TO THE VILLAGE
AGAIN, EH?" SNAPPED MADGE

DAPHNE BEGAN TO SENSE SHE WAS NO
LONGER ALONE.....

ANGELA ADDRESSED THE
MEMBERS OF THE CROCHET
CLUB ON HER PROPOSALS FOR
DEALING WITH LATECOMERS

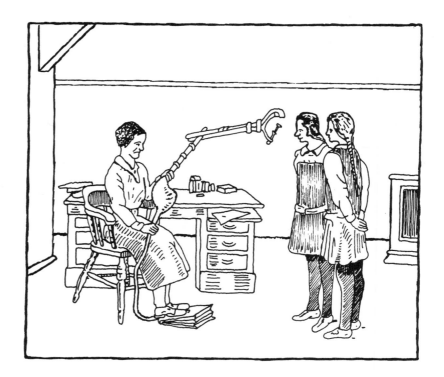

MISS FROBISHER MADE A POINT OF
THREATENING NEW ARRIVALS
WITH "THE NOSE TWEAKER"

DEIDRE POINTED OUT HER SUPPLY OF HASHISH
FOR THE AUTUMN TERM

AFTER TEA, MONICA WAS FORCED TO
ENACT THE GRIM RITUAL OF
"COUNTING THE STUMPS"

MIRANDA HAD STUMBLED UPON OUR
SUPPLY OF BEARDS.......

GLADYS HAD NOT REALIZED THAT VIRGINIA
WAS UNABLE TO ACCEPT DEFEAT GRACEFULLY

PHYLLIS REALIZED ALMOST INSTINCTIVELY
THAT IT WAS JUST A PIECE OF PAPER

"THAT IS MR. SMOLLET'S EYEBROW!"
DECLARED JANEY

"I THINK I KNOW HOW TO THANK OLD
BRINKLAID FOR NOT ALLOWING US
TO HOLD THE JITTERBUG FESTIVAL
IN OUR DORM" ANNOUNCED LUCY

I BEGAN TO SUSPECT THAT
MIRIAM WAS DELIBERATELY
SETTING OUT TO ANNOY ME

WAY
OUT
WEST

PECOS BILL HAD A "THING"
ABOUT HOUSEHOLD DUST.....

"I PRUNE MY CHRYSANTHEMUMS THIS-A-WAY...."

JEDSON WAS NOTED FOR HIS WITHERING
SIDELONG GLANCES

"I KEEP MY BAGELS IN HERE"
WHISPERED THE DESPERADO

"THE WAY I FIGGER IT – TRUTH IS
UN-TRUTH INSOFAR AS THERE
BELONGS TO IT THE RESERVOIR OF
THE NOT-YET-REVEALED, THE
UN-UNCOVERED IN THE SENSE OF
CONCEALMENT" REASONED M^cTAGGART

YOUNG HANK ENTERTAINED THE BOYS
WITH A FINE DISPLAY OF SMOULDERING

AT THE GIVEN SIGNAL, MRS BOTHAM
POPPED OUT FROM THE CONCEALED
LINING AND BLASTED THE RATTLER

IT WAS TOM'S FIRST BRUSH
WITH MODERNISM

Professions of the Old West

No. 2

The Dentist

WILD BILL WAS KNOWN TO GO TO EXTRA-
ORDINARY LENGTHS TO CATCH "THE LUCY
SHOW" REPEATS ON CHANNEL SIX

VANCE LIVED IN CONSTANT FEAR
OF LOSING HIS WRISTWATCH....

"I STUB MY CIGARS OUT........ THERE!"
SNORTED THE TEXAN

"BUT SURELY, LANGUAGE IS NOT
DEFINED FOR US AS AN ARRANGE-
MENT FULFILLING A DEFINITE
PURPOSE...." STAMMERED JED

FRUITS OF THE WORLD
IN
DANGER

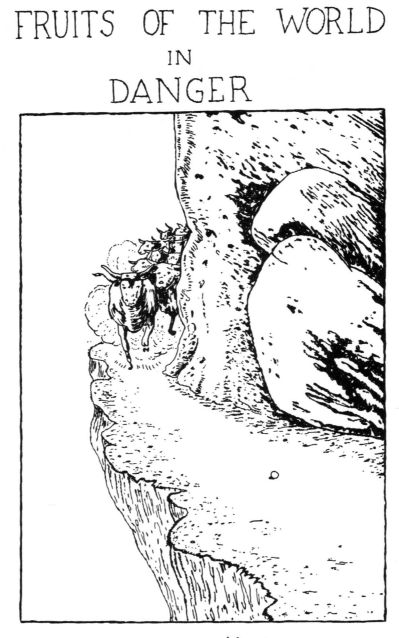

Number 10   The Apricot

IT WAS THE HALITOSIS KID.....

"I'VE CALLED ABOUT THE POST OF ASSISTANT
MILLINER" DRAWLED DEKE

YOUNG ERIC HAD PREPARED HIMSELF FOR
ALMOST ANY EMERGENCY....

PANCHO'S SLEEPING ARRANGEMENTS WERE
THE TALK OF THE BUNKHOUSE

" SO YOU SEE, BOYS — WHAT A PICTURE MUST
HAVE IN COMMON WITH REALITY, IN ORDER
TO BE ABLE TO DEPICT IT — CORRECTLY OR
INCORRECTLY — IN THE WAY IT DOES, IS
ITS PICTORIAL FORM" EXPLAINED TEX

SETH TOOK HIS TEA AT SEVEN ON THE DOT

"I MAKE A LIVING PEDDLING
DANDRUFF" SNORTED THE
OLD TIMER

McGUIRE SEEMED TO HAVE RIDDEN
INTO A TRAP......

THE LOMAX BOYS KEPT UP AN ALL-NIGHT
VIGIL ON THE NOUGAT

HE WAS FORCED TO ENDURE TERRIBLE
IMPERSONATIONS OF ANNETTE FUNICELLO

"TO ME THE WINDOW IS STILL A
SYMBOLICALLY LOADED MOTIF"
DRAWLED CODY

"WE DON'T HOLD WITH PUCCINI
AT THE LAZY Z," SNARLED TEX

TOM TRIED OUT THE NEW BULLET

"I WHITTLE THESE!" BLURTED CRAIG

SETH'S SNOOD WAS THE ENVY
OF THE BOYS IN THE BUNKHOUSE

"MISTER...JES KEEP YOUR JUNGIAN
ANALYSIS TO YO'SELF....YOU HEAR?"
GROWLED MRS. BOTHAM

"WE'LL HAVE NO ALLITERATION IN THIS
HERE BUNKHOUSE!" SNORTED McCULLOCH

"TAKE A TIP FROM ME, YOUNG FELLER—
ALWAYS CARRY A SPARE GOATEE...."

GRADUALLY I BEGAN TO CONCUR
WITH HIS POINT OF VIEW

I WAS STILL NOT ENTIRELY
HAPPY WITH THE SLEEPING
ARRANGEMENTS...

LEON'S FORTH BRIDGE WAS BUT ONE
OF THE MANY HIGHLIGHTS OF
THAT WEEKEND IN TULSA

"I KNOW IT'S A BAD DRAWING,
BUT THIS IS SUPPOSED TO BE
A STAR" GRUMBLED NED DRYLY

UNLUCKY MEMBERS OF THE POSSE
WERE PERMITTED ONLY THE
BRIEFEST GLIMPSE OF TIM'S ELBOW...

THE BARTENDER WAS A MOODY,
UNPREDICTABLE BELGIAN, WHOSE
KNOWLEDGE OF MARQUETRY WAS
RARELY, IF EVER, CALLED INTO QUESTION

AS HE REACHED THE FINAL
PARAGRAPH OF HIS MARRIAGE
PROPOSAL, BILLY NOTICED THAT
RUTH WAS NO LONGER THERE

HANK HAD SPOTTED THE
GOUDA AGAIN

BRENDA'S WEEKEND BREAK
IN TUCSON HAD CLEARLY
BEEN PIVOTAL

THERE WAS ALWAYS AN UNSEEMLY
RUSH FOR SEATS AT THE
CROCHET SEMINAR

TEX SPENT MANY LONG
HOURS CONTEMPLATING
THE CAMEMBERT

THE TWO MEN WERE IN AGREEMENT
—IT WAS A WORK OF SOME MERIT

THE TWO MEN WERE IN AGREEMENT
—IT WAS A WORK WITHOUT MERIT

IT WAS HORRIBLE. FROM MY VANTAGE POINT
I COULD SEE THE STRUGGLING FIGURES
BEING CARTED INTO PROFESSOR TREMBO'S
STRUCTURALIST FILM SEMINAR

"AH YES, MR. WRIGGLESWORTH — IT'S ABOUT
THIS......AHEM.....FIRST DRAFT OF YOUR
NOVEL" SPLUTTERED MR. SCELPE

HE TOOK HER IN HIS ARMS AND
GENTLY SQUEEZED HER GOATEE

"SO YOU'RE THE MYOPIC MULDONI BOYS
FROM CHICAGO, EH?" SPAT LANNIGAN

HE WAS NOT THE MAN SHE HAD
LOVED THAT EVENING IN
BRIDGEPORT......

GUSTAV'S NEON WIMPLE WAS CLEARLY
FAILING TO IMPRESS THELMA

"SOME ARE HAM AND SOME ARE CHEESE
AND PICKLE" CONFIDED PANDOWSKI

HE WAS FROM BROOKLYN ALL RIGHT

THE MANAGER WAS STRONGLY
RECOMMENDING THE SCROD

"NOW WHICH ONE OF YOU IS MRS. BLOYARD?"
ASKED THE INSPECTOR

THE INSURANCE SALESMAN MOVED IN
BRANDISHING HIS POLICIES

HARRY AND HIS TRICK FINGER WERE
BEGINNING TO BECOME TIRESOME
NOTED MASSINGTON

That Fateful Encounter

"NOW THIS MAY LOOK LIKE AN ORDINARY
NOSE...." BEGAN THE TRAVELLER

EAKINS SPENT MOST OF
THANKSGIVING WORKING ON
HIS OIL DRUM TECHNIQUE

"THAT'S L-E-P-A-G-E WITH AN E,"
CORRECTED THE DOORMAN

AS THE EVENING WORE ON I BEGAN
TO SUSPECT THAT I WAS IN THE
PRESENCE OF A DESPERATE MAN...

"THE GAME'S UP, MRS. SO-CALLED
RAMSTED!" BARKED INSPECTOR THRUMM

YOUNG ROBERTS COULD NOT FACE ANOTHER MOUSSAKA

SENSING AN IMMINENT PROPOSAL
OF MARRIAGE, INGRID SWITCHED
DWIGHT'S SCOTCH FOR A DOUBLE
CURARE ON THE ROCKS

"ONLY A PRIVILEGED FEW ARE
ALLOWED TO TOUCH MY HUSKS"
WHISPERED CURTIS

CHESTER'S DEFINITION OF
"DEBONAIR" DID NOT ENTIRELY
CORRESPOND WITH THAT
HELD BY CLARISSA

GREAT
CULINARY
DISASTERS
OF OUR
TIME

CHICKEN MARYLAND, WEMBLEY 2/14/53

STEWED FIGS AMERICAN STYLE —
ANTWERP, NOVEMBER 3, 1974

ASPARAGUS IN MUSTARD SAUCE, UTRECHT,
APRIL 11, 1949

FEGATO ALLA VENEZIANA, DUSSELDORF,
NOVEMBER 21, 1928

FILETS DE CANETON AU CHERRY MARNIER
(POUR 2 PERSONNES), NEWPORT PAGNELL,
FEBRUARY 3, 1973

GRATIN DE LANGOUSTE À LA NORMANDE,
EDINBURGH   8/14/58

CAULIFLOWER POLONAISE, NEW CROSS,
SOUTH LONDON, SEPTEMBER 23, 1976

PLAT DU JOUR, CANAL STREET,
NEW YORK, APRIL 16 & 17, 1963

HOT DOG-ZUCCHINI COMBO,
BELGRADE 2/2/68

CHICKEN FRIED RICE, MERTHYR TYDFIL,
SEPTEMBER 26, 1971

GLADYS TOOK HER HIGHBALLS
VERY SERIOUSLY

BALLANTINE CALCULATED THAT HE WAS
APPROACHING THE SAUERKRAUT AT AN
APPROXIMATE VELOCITY OF 78.6 M.P.H

ASKING SIMON TO LEND A HAND
IN THE KITCHEN WAS ALWAYS
A BIG MISTAKE...

"I'M AFRAID IT LOOKS LIKE
ANOTHER MASSIVE, OVERCOOKED
OMELETTE!" BARKED SNODE

THE SHADOW OVER DRINGFIELD

"I HOPE YOU CAN EXPLAIN THAT MOUND OF PEANUT HUSKS IN MY BEDROOM!" SNAPPED GATTING

WITH AN AIR OF WEARIED RESIGNATION
PROFESSOR COOMBES TUCKED THE ESSAY
BACK INTO MY BEARD

"WHEN THIS IS SWITCHED ON, YOUR PANTS
WILL BE CLEANED AND PRESSED EVERY
TWO MINUTES" SNAPPED TOWLE

THE LADS HAD A WAY OF DEALING
WITH BORING OLD RELATIVES

AS THE AFTERNOON WORE ON I BEGAN TO
SUSPECT THAT MR PHELPORT WAS INDEED
KEEPING SOMETHING FROM ME

YOUNG TALBOT STOOD UP AND WITH A
SHRIEK OF TRIUMPH WHISKED OFF HIS
BOATER TO REVEAL THE FORBIDDEN
POMPADOUR......

THERE WAS STILL MUCH TO
LEARN ABOUT SZECHUAN
CUISINE

"THERE'S ONLY ONE WAY TO
EAT WHELKS" HISSED GREIG

"IF THERE HAS BEEN A MISHAP ON THE SPORTS
FIELD THEN NATURALLY I WANT TO BE THE
FIRST TO KNOW" MUMBLED THE HEADMASTER

SUNDAYS CAME AROUND WITH
DEPRESSING REGULARITY

"I'M AFRAID IT'S GRIM NEWS,
SANDY— THE VICE-CONSUL
INTENDS TO BAN THE
WEARING OF WIMPLES
AFTER 7:15 P.M"

IT WAS A DEVICE FOR TURNING SCHOOL MEALS
BACK INTO FOOD

HE HAD BEEN CAUGHT USING THE
FORBIDDEN "HEAD PEN" AGAIN.......

THE DEAN WASN'T THERE ANYMORE

IT WAS PRECISELY SIX-FIFTEEN

AFTER LIGHTS OUT, SMYTHE WOULD TAP
OUT A CHAPTER OF "PRIDE & PREJUDICE"
IN MORSE CODE FOR THE LADS
IN DORMITORY 'K'....

THURSDAYS WERE
SET ASIDE FOR PLAITING

"SO YOU'VE ALMOST PERFECTED YOUR
INVISIBLE RAY, EH WILKINS?"

EVERY OTHER WEDNESDAY THE LADS
WERE ALLOWED AN EXTRA RATION

"THIS BEARD OF YOURS SEEMS TO BE
FASHIONED FROM CORK," SNAPPED BLY

IT WAS GOING TO BE THE USUAL
DULL CHRISTMAS

IT WAS CLEARLY THE BELGIAN WHO
WAS TAMPERING WITH THE PILCHARDS

I WAS NOT TO FORGET MY FIRST
DETENTION WITH MR. BLISWORTH

BOYS WHO HAD FORGOTTEN THEIR
PROTRACTORS WERE SUBJECTED TO
MR LLOYD'S WALNUT ORDEAL

THE BEST PART OF THE DAY WAS THE
SINGALONG ROUND THE SMOULDERING
REMAINS OF THE SCOUTMASTER'S
LUGGAGE ...

WE WERE BEGINNING TO HAVE
OUR DOUBTS ABOUT THE NEW
GIRL, HELGA SCHUMTRAUB...

HAPPY HOUR AT BEAMINSTER HALL
ALWAYS MEANT SOMETHING
RATHER SPECIAL FOR THE THIRD
EARL OF BEAUFORD

DURING MY ABSENCE I COULD SEE
THAT GRUNCHESTER HALL HAD
BEEN RESTORED TO ITS
FORMER GLORY

I HAD DRAWN THE SHORT STRAW.
I WAS TO SPEND THE HALF-TERM
WITH UNCLE GILBERT

"SO, YOU SEE, IT IS POSSIBLE TO REDUCE
YOUR FATHER'S UNWIELDY JAZZ COLLECTION
DOWN TO THIS BASIC FORM..." EXPLAINED TIM

THE HOLIDAY BEGAN WITH ANOTHER
PETTY FAMILY SQUABBLE

THERE WAS REALLY NOTHING
QUITE LIKE HOME COOKING

EDGAR HAD ATTENDED MANY
A POETRY EVENING

"SO YOU FOUND THE BUTTER,
THEN?" GRUNTED KLAUS

"I THOUGHT WE HAD AGREED NOT TO DISCUSS
YOUR HUSBAND" SNAPPED CELIA

I LIKED TO THINK THAT MY
RELATIONSHIP WITH IRMA
WAS RATHER SPECIAL

WHEN UNCLE NORMAN BEGAN TO
REMINISCE ABOUT THE
SIXTIES, TIM AND I WERE
FORCED TO PUT PLAN 'B'
INTO OPERATION

HE SEEMED TO THINK I HAD
NEVER SWEPT A FLOOR BEFORE

WE CELEBRATED FATHER'S BIRTHDAY
IN THE TRADITIONAL MANNER

"THERE ARE MANY THINGS TO ADMIRE
IN THIS OLD WORLD, BUT A SINGING
STOCKBROKER IS NOT ONE OF THEM..."
NOTED THE SAGE

I NEVER FULLY RECOVERED FROM THE
APPALLING SHOCK OF DISCOVERING MY
FATHER'S COLLECTION OF FLEETWOOD
MAC ALBUMS...

FOR MALCOLM, EDNA WOULD
CONTINUE TO REMAIN AN ENIGMA

ERIC WAS NOW BEGINNING TO WISH HE'D
RETURNED HIS OVERDUE LIBRARY BOOKS

THROUGHOUT THAT DISMAL SUMMER I
REMAINED STEADFASTLY IMPERVIOUS
TO HIS MERRYMAKING

"I KNEW IT WAS A MISTAKE TO
ORDER THE BOURRIDE OF BRILL
AND MONKFISH" HISSED SCRUTON

THE TWINS WERE NOT NOTED FOR
THEIR LOVE OF FRESH VEGETABLES

I KNEW THERE WAS SOMETHING
SLIGHTLY DISCONCERTING ABOUT
JULIAN, BUT HIS CAREER
PROSPECTS WERE EXCELLENT

SIXTEEN HOURS IN THE CELLAR BROUGHT
US TO OUR SENSES. WE AGREED TO STAY
AWAKE DURING THE REMAINING SLIDES
OF MR. BLUM'S DUTCH HIKING HOLIDAY

WITH DEADLY ACCURACY, ROBIN'S
FLASHLIGHT PICKED OUT THE
HIDDEN GOURDS

THERE WERE TIMES WHEN I BEGAN
TO TIRE OF POLISHING MR. THRONGUE

AS COLLECTIONS OF TEETH GO, IT
WAS CERTAINLY IMPRESSIVE

IT WAS NOT TOO LONG
BEFORE WE BEGAN TO
ORGANIZE REGULAR MEETINGS

UNFORTUNATELY ROBIN SEEMED
TO HAVE SLIPPED INTO FESTIVE
MODE ONCE AGAIN...

"I'D LIKE YOU TO MEET THE FUTURE MRS. BOSWORTH" ANNOUNCED SNOAD